W9-CJX-888

613
M65

Michael Morcombe's
BIRDS OF AUSTRALIA

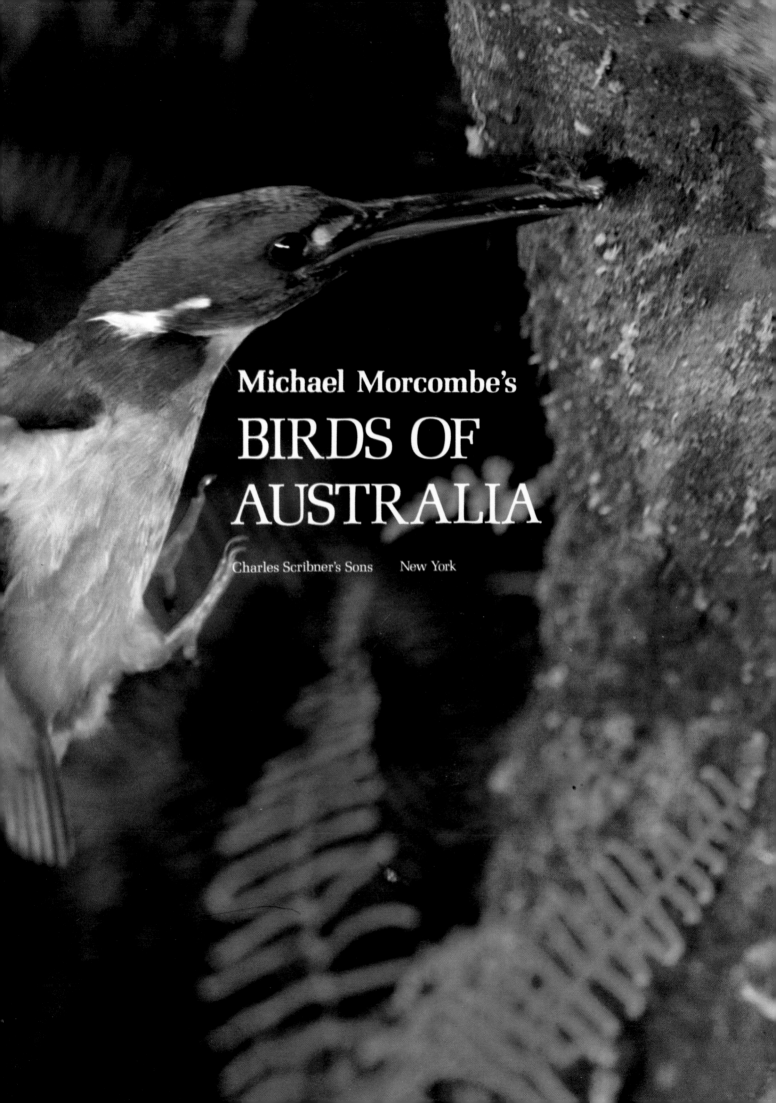

Michael Morcombe's
BIRDS OF AUSTRALIA

Charles Scribner's Sons   New York

CONTENTS

CHAPTER ONE   Birds of the Coastal Rainforests   5

CHAPTER TWO   Honeyeaters   15

CHAPTER THREE   Australian Robins   20

CHAPTER FOUR   Birds of the Dry Inland   27

CHAPTER FIVE   Parrots   34

CHAPTER SIX   Birds of Prey   42

CHAPTER SEVEN   Fairy Wrens   46

CHAPTER EIGHT   Birds of Rivers, Swamps and Tropical Grasslands   50

CHAPTER NINE   Birds of Ocean, Seashore and Lakes   54

CHAPTER TEN   Birds of Forests and Woodlands   58

Australian Bird Families   66–7

Techniques for Bird Photography   68

Acknowledgments   69

Distribution of Birds   70

Selected Bibliography   80

Index   80

1 3 5 7 9 11 13 15 17 19 I/C 20 18 16 14 12 10 8 6 4 2

First published 1971 by Lansdowne Press, Melbourne, Australia

Printed in Hong Kong Library of Congress Catalog Card Number 73-7166

SBN 684-13553-1 (cloth)

BIRDS OF THE COASTAL RAINFORESTS

Australia's tropical and sub-tropical jungles are located principally along the north-eastern coastline, extending in isolated pockets around the tropical northern coastline to the Kimberleys of Western Australia. Southwards, rainforests occur in small patches to eastern Victoria.

The birds of these rainforests are, for the most part, quite distinct from those of other Australian forests. Many are species whose true home is New Guinea and adjacent tropical islands. The Yellow-breasted Sunbird occurs in New Guinea, the Celebes and the Solomon Islands, but in Australia is found only in the jungles of far north-eastern Queensland; the Azure Kingfisher is in New Guinea, the Moluccas and Solomon Islands; the Great Palm Cockatoo of New Guinea may be seen, in Australia, only in jungles at the tip of Cape York Peninsula.

Australia's bowerbirds are members of a fascinating group centred upon the mountains of New Guinea. The north Queensland jungles have three species, the Paradise Rifle-bird, the Prince Albert Rifle-bird and the Queen Victoria Rifle-bird, belonging to the magnificent bird-of-paradise family, which has its stronghold in New Guinea and neighbouring islands. Within Australia, it is only in the comparatively small areas of rainforest that we have this glimpse of the exotic splendour of the jungle birds of New Guinea.

Azure Kingfishers, *Alcyone azurea*, are barely eight inches in length. They inhabit creeks and rivers of coastal eastern and northern Australia, often in rainforest country. The prey, mainly small fish, frogs and crustaceans, is captured in a plunging dive from a perch overhanging the water.

Below
The ringing whipcrack call of the Eastern Whipbird, *Psophodes olivaceus*, is one of the dominant sounds of jungles and densely vegetated gullies from north-eastern Queensland to Victoria. The birds, shy and elusive, are usually hard to see as they search among fallen leaves and other debris of the forest floor. Two eggs, bluish with markings of black and lavender, are laid in a nest well hidden in a tangle of vines or undergrowth.

Right
Australia's one species of the sunbird family (*Nectariniidae*), the Yellow-breasted Sunbird, *Cyrtostomus frenatus*, is restricted within Australia to north-eastern Queensland. It often hovers, hummingbird-like, in front of a flower where it will feed on nectar and small insects. Shown flying up to the large pendant nest is the female; the male has a deep blue throat. The two or three eggs are grey-green, spotted with brown.

Right
The flycatchers' deep cup-shaped nest, placed as low as three feet or as high as thirty, is covered with green moss so that, from some distance, it cannot be distinguished from the innumerable lumps and tangles of similar moss that festoon the jungle trees. The two or three eggs are white, finely spotted with red.

Left
Black-faced Flycatchers, *Monarcha melanopsis*, are birds of the rainforests of coastal eastern Australia. The flycatchers are seen most often in the forest canopy, where they take insects in flight and on the foliage.

Below
Incubation is shared by male and female, whose plumage appears identical. When the eggs hatch the flycatchers are kept busy bringing insects, though while the young are very small one or other of the parents is usually on the nest.

Rarely seen, and photographed on two or three occasions only, the Rufous Scrub-bird, *Atrichornis rufescens*, has a distribution restricted to mountain-top rainforests of south-eastern Queensland and north-eastern New South Wales. An accomplished mimic and ventriloquist, the male calls loudly from dense thickets around the boundary of his territory, fluttering his wings in agitation or defiance if another male appears nearby.

Below
The Golden Bower-bird, *Priondura newtoniana*, which inhabits mountainous parts of north-eastern Queensland, is the smallest of the bower-birds of Australia and New Guinea, yet builds a massive bower up to nine feet high. Bowers are built to attract females for courtship and mating; here the male visits his display perch to renew and rearrange the decoration of mosses and small jungle flowers.

Right
With long tail a restless dancing patch of bright colour in the green gloom of the jungle, a Rufous Fantail, *Rhipidura rufifrons*, comes to its neat 'wine-glass' nest. This small bird of the flycatcher family favours rainforests and fern gullies, and occurs in suitable habitat around Australia's northern and eastern coasts. It is a summer visitor in the south-east. The two or three eggs are buff-coloured with the brown spots forming a band around the larger end.

Below
Yellow-throated Scrub-wrens, *Sericornis lathami*, have a coastal distribution from north-eastern Queensland to eastern Victoria. Known also as 'Devil-birds' because they are always found in the darkest parts of the rainforest where they search among litter and mossy logs, the scrub-wrens build a suspended nest that may be three feet in length.

1

HONEYEATERS

Honeyeaters, family *Meliphagidae*, are found chiefly in Australia and New Guinea, but extend also to the Solomon Islands, New Zealand, the Moluccas, Micronesia, Polynesia and Hawaii. There are some 160 species, most of which have slender, down-curved and usually quite long beaks. Their tongues are specially adapted for taking nectar from flowers, being extensile and brushlike; often the sides of the long tongue curl upwards to form a tube through which nectar and nectar-eating insects are sucked into the throat.

Sixty-nine species of honeyeaters occur within Australia, and it is believed that these, feeding constantly at gum blossoms and the flowers of other trees and shrubs, not only serve as pollinators, but also have caused many plants to evolve flowers designed exclusively for transfer of pollen from flower to flower by birds. Such flowers usually provide a perch for the bird (on top of a banksia spike, or on the red stem of a kangaroo-paw), and generally are brightly coloured, with a tendency to be stiff and strong to withstand probing, sharp-pointed beaks.

Honeyeaters may be seen in almost every part of Australia, though fewer species inhabit regions of sparse vegetation, such as the central deserts.

The Yellow-plumed Honeyeater, *Meliphaga ornata*, lives in the mallee districts of western New South Wales, north-western Victoria and South Australia, and the south-west woodlands country of Western Australia. They build a fragile open cup nest of grasses in the outer foliage of a small tree. Active birds before sunrise, they attract attention with their upward flights and loud calls. They are very aggressive, and will chase birds away from trees in which they are feeding.　　*Left and below*

Left
A male Western Spinebill, *Acanthorhynchus superciliosus*, probing the flowers of a Scarlet Regelia shrub will carry its pollen daubed on plumage around his face.

Below
A female Western Spinebill feeding at a *Grevillea wilsonii* shrub. On her forehead she carries a patch of pollen where the long style (which both places and receives pollen at different stages in the life of the flower) touches as she pushes her beak into the curved crimson perianth.

Right
From its perch on a *Banksia attenuata* spike a Yellow-throated Miner, *Myzantha flavigula*, probes among the close-packed flowers. This honeyeater is very widespread through inland Australia in open forest and dry scrublands. Some authorities consider the very similar Dusky Miner to be a geographic race of the Yellow-throated, one form merging with the other.

This Yellow-faced Honeyeater, _Meliphaga chrysops_, seeking nectar at a Christmas Bell, will carry pollen from plant to plant—the bird must thrust its head deep into the flower, brushing the style and pollen-covered anthers; the plant's stiff stems provide a very convenient perch. This honeyeater occurs in eastern Australia and Tasmania.

Below
A Western Spinebill lands in a clump of Red-and-green Kangaroo-paws. Though honeyeaters feed extensively upon nectar they inevitably take many minute insects and spiders along with the nectar; Spinebills are often seen capturing larger insects in the air. This is a common bird in forests and woodlands in south-western Australia.

Right
Flowers which have evolved for pollination by birds usually have strong stems and stiff wiry flower structure as evident in the banksias with their brush-like texture. The New Holland Honeyeater, also called Yellow-winged Honeyeater, has a coastal distribution from southern Queensland through New South Wales and Victoria to South Australia and Tasmania; it also occurs in south-western Australia.

AUSTRALIAN ROBINS

The Australian robins belong to the Old World Fly-catchers family, *Muscicapidae*, but unlike the typical flycatchers which form part of this family, the robins (sub-family *Muscicapinae*) do not usually capture insects in the air. They sit motionless, but for an occasional flick of the wings, on a perch, or clinging to the side of a treetrunk, and drop to the ground to capture their prey.

There are five species with red or pink breasts, some six species with extensive areas of bright yellow, and a number of less colourful birds including the White-breasted Robin, the Dusky Robin, the Hooded Robin and others.

Characteristics of the Old World Flycatcher family include relatively weak legs and feet (being used only for perching), ten primaries in the wings, and pronounced bristles at the base of the upper mandible. Nests are open, cup-shaped structures, which in the case of the robins are beautifully camouflaged with bark, mosses, and lichen, bound and matted with spider-webs.

The Australian robins occupy a wide variety of habitats, from Alpine (Flame Robin) to tropical mangrove swamps (Buff-sided Robin); from rainforests (White-faced Robin, Rose Robin, Northern Yellow Robin) to semi-desert (Red-capped and Hooded Robins), while the Dusky Robin is confined to Tasmania and islands of Bass Strait, and the White-breasted Robin is found only in south-western Australia.

Right
When touched by the feet of the flying Scarlet Robin the nest becomes filled with wide-open, brightly coloured beaks. Until that moment the young lie still, relying upon their protective coloration to escape detection by predators.
Below
A brilliantly coloured male Flame Robin, *Petroica phoenicea*, joins his mate at a nest tucked behind a projecting piece of bark. Confined to Tasmania and south-eastern Australia they spread out from mountains and heavy forests to more open plains after nesting.

Below
Courtship feeding, the male bringing gifts of food for the female, is common among the robins. During incubation, he feeds his mate at the nest and she accepts with much agitated fluttering of wings. Red-capped Robins, *Petroica goodenovii*, have an almost Australia-wide distribution, favouring dry inland areas, but avoiding the tropical north; they are also absent from Tasmania.

Right
Landing with wings out the male Red-capped Robin reveals the conspicuous white wing markings which are also seen on Scarlet and Flame Robins; however, this is the only species with a red forehead patch. The nest is very effectively camouflaged with green mosses, lichen and pieces of bark. The two or three eggs are pale blue-green spotted with brown and grey.

Over left
Isolated in the coastal south-western corner of the continent, Western Yellow Robins, *Eopsaltria griseogularis*, have gradually evolved a plumage pattern slightly different to that of the Southern Yellow Robins of south-eastern Australia; there is a broad grey breast band between white throat and yellow abdomen. Male and female have similar plumage.

Over right
Yellow robins inhabit coastal eastern Australia from Victoria northwards into tropical Queensland; however, towards the north the robins become progressively more richly coloured, a little larger in size, and are known as Northern Yellow Robins, *Eopsaltria chrysorrhoa*. Because there is no clear-cut demarcation these northern birds are now considered to be a sub-species of the Southern Yellow Robin.

BIRDS OF THE DRY INLAND

Vast tracts of the Australian continent are desert, or so dry that only low harsh grasses and scattered, stunted mulga bushes can survive. Yet these inhospitable expanses of sand dunes, barren rocky ranges and sparse scrub have a wealth of bird life.

The birds of the centre are able to survive partly because they are nomadic, travelling great distances to avoid drought, then settling to breed wherever good seasonal rains or a localized but heavy thunderstorm downpour has rejuvenated the landscape. A month or two after rain the soil can be carpeted with fresh grass and brightened with drifts of wildflowers; birds are everywhere, many already involved in nest building or rearing young. But twelve months later the same scene will probably be bare and seemingly lifeless. None but a few sedentary birds remain. During one drought period a count of birds at Ayers Rock totalled thirty species; two months later, after several inches of rain had fallen, there were more than sixty species, many of which were beginning to breed. For this reason it is essential, if planning to visit any arid inland district in search of birds, to take seasonal conditions into account, preferably arriving a month or two after good rains have fallen.

Below
The Orange Chat, *Epthianura aurifrons*, is a bird of the open, sparsely-vegetated semi-arid interior.
Left
A Ground Cuckoo-Shrike, *Pteropodocys maxima*, about to settle onto its eggs. These birds spend much of their time in small flocks on the ground in mulga scrub and sparsely timbered country.

Orange wings flash against sky and treetops as a Rainbow Bird twists and turns in pursuit of dragonflies and other fast-flying insects, then glides back to its perch on a dead limb. The nest is a tunnel drilled into the ground. The Rainbow Bird, *Merops ornatus*, Australia's only representative of the bee-eater group, occurs almost throughout Australia, avoiding only the heavy forests of the south-east and south-west. It is migratory over most of its range, those birds which nest in southern Australia in summer moving northwards for the winter.

Landing at its nest in a low pink-flowered
mulla-mulla bush a male Crimson Chat,
Epthianura tricolor, brings food for the
ever-hungry young; he also assists with
incubation. This chat inhabits inland
Australia from Queensland, New South
Wales and Victoria through Central
Australia to Western Australia. Crimson
Chats tend to be nomadic, wandering,
often in large flocks, wherever conditions
are best. A nest is made in a low, dense
bush, and three or four eggs, white
spotted with red and purple, are laid.
Below
The Orange Chat ranges from western
Queensland and New South Wales,
north-western Victoria, through South
Australia and Central Australia to the
north-west coast of Western Australia. Its
favoured habitats include samphire flats
around inland salt lakes and the margins of
marine marshes, where the small cup-
shaped nest is concealed in a low bush.

Right
Flying into its nest tunnel the Red-backed
Kingfisher, *Halcyon pyrrhopygia*, shows
the chestnut brown of its lower back and
tail coverts. This species is commonly
encountered far from water, inhabiting the
driest regions, and ranging across the
continent from inland New South Wales
to the north-western coast.
Below
The Red-backed Kingfisher drills a tunnel
into the bank of a dry creek or into a
termite nest; four or five rounded white
eggs are laid in the terminal chamber.
When the shadow of the flying bird
darkens the tunnel entrance the young
rush forward to take whatever small
reptile, or other prey, is presented in the
kingfisher's beak.

32

PARROTS

Australia's many colourful parrots, cockatoos and lorikeets together make up one of the best-known and most distinctive of bird groups. The Order Psittaciformes contains three families which share the distinguishing parrot features, including short rounded bill with hinged and movable upper mandible, nostrils set in a fleshy cere at the base of the bill, and thick prehensile tongue. Their feet have two forward and two backward-pointing toes, and their plumage contains powder-down feathers, the tips of which steadily disintegrate to form a powder used in dressing the plumage.

The lorikeets, family *Loriidae*, are brush-tongued birds that feed largely upon the nectar of flowering trees and shrubs, mainly in eucalypt forests; the family includes some brilliantly plumaged birds such as the Rainbow Lorikeet.

Cockatoos, family *Cacatuidae*, the largest of Australia's parrot-like birds, have a conspicuous movable crest, often brightly coloured, which frequently is raised immediately after the birds alight, or when they are alarmed, or excited.

The third family, *Psittacidae*, contains those many parrot-like birds not having the distinguishing features of lorikeets or cockatoos; among the parrots, perhaps more than in any other Australian bird group, the plumage is brilliant, varied, often gaudy in colour, making this a truly spectacular segment of Australian birdlife.

Below left
Scaly-breasted Lorikeets, *Trichoglossus chlorolepidotus*, inhabit the eastern coast from north-eastern Queensland to Sydney. These small nectar-eating birds are nomadic, wandering wherever trees and shrubs are in flower. Their nest is a hollow limb, usually at a considerable height; two or three oval white eggs are laid.

Right
The Turquoise Parrot, *Neophema pulchella*, is now a rare species and is found only in scattered small areas of open forest and timbered grassland from south-eastern Queensland to Victoria.

3

Below left to right
The swift flight of a Crimson Rosella is
stopped by the 1/7000th of a second
flashes of light from an electronic flash
triggered by the camera's shutter. With the
fast action frozen, it is possible to see
details which to the human eye are but a
blur of movement. Sharply defined are the
positions of wings, tail and feet as the bird
sweeps in to a landing, then dives away
after feeding its young in the hollow; it is
possible to study the action of flight
feathers and tail as they spread to check
the bird's speed of landing, or propel it
away from the tree. The Crimson Rosella,
Platycercus elegans, inhabits coastal forests
and ranges from north-eastern Queensland
to South Australia.

Far left
Purple-crowned Lorikeets, *Glossopsitta porphyrocephala*, at the entrance of their nest hollow in a high branch of a eucalypt, are among the smallest Australian parrots, being only six inches in length. These nectar-eating birds follow the flowering of the eucalypts. They frequent both heavy forest and mallee country, and occur in south-eastern and south-western Australia.

Left
A pair of Rainbow Lorikeets look cautiously at the camera lens protruding from the hide before entering the hollow. After feeding the young they sit preening their feathers, one showing the crimson of its under-wings, before flying off. Rainbow Lorikeets, *Trichoglossus haematodus*, have a predominantly coastal distribution from north-east Queensland to South Australia and Tasmania, inhabiting rainforests, sclerophyll forests and woodlands.

Left
Diving from its nest hollow in an old eucalypt a Galah shows the graceful form and beauty of plumage that make it one of the most attractive of Australia's common birds. Shown here is the Western Australian sub-species, *Eolophus roseicapillus assimilis*, which has the ring around the eye white instead of dusky crimson, and subtle differences in plumage colour.

Below
A male Western Rosella twists into flight from where he has been clinging at the rim of the nest hollow; his widespread tail has a feather bent by the sudden action. The less colourful female, wings slightly raised in alarm, waits to feed the four or five young inside the hollow. The Western Rosella, *Platycercus icterotis*, is found only in south-western Australia. It prefers open forest, woodlands and lightly timbered grasslands.

Right
Diving from its nest hollow in the side of a treetrunk a Twenty-eight Parrot, *Barnardius zonarius semitorquatus*, is caught in a moment of spectacular action. Named for its distinctive double-noted call, it is found only in the forested south-western corner of the continent.

Below left to right
Diving away from its nest hollow in a high branch of a tall eucalypt a male Red-capped Parrot, *Purpureicephalus spurius*, shows its rich gaudy plumage. The high speed electronic flash captured wing and tail action, revealing details of bird flight too fast to be seen, as well as showing that in flight a bird can have superior beauty of plumage pattern and colour than when perched. This parrot inhabits forests and woodlands of south-western Australia.

The Cockatiel, *Nymphicus hollandicus*, is found throughout the interior of Australia in open country, usually in the vicinity of creeks and waterholes. In arid regions these birds take advantage of rain at almost any time of the year to breed.

Bottom left to right
A male Mulga Parrot, *Psephotus varius*, lands at its nest hollow. It is distributed from western New South Wales through Central Australia and Western Australia and inhabits arid mulga and mallee scrub country, being most often seen near inland lakes and waterholes.

Sulphur-crested Cockatoos, *Cacatua galerita*, nest in a hollow in a large eucalypt high above the ground. Two or three white eggs are laid. The young cockatoos remain in the nest for approximately six weeks after hatching. Sulphur-crested Cockatoos range from the Kimberleys of the far north-west around northern and eastern coasts to the south-east and Tasmania.

Right
A Port Lincoln Parrot, *Barnardius zonarius* rushing from its hollow, displays the yellow abdomen which distinguishes it from the similar Twenty-eight Parrot, which is entirely green below. This species is widely distributed in southern, central and western parts of the continent, extending as far to the east as Eyre Peninsula.

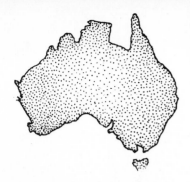

BIRDS OF PREY

Nocturnal and diurnal birds of prey may be encountered in almost every part of Australia. There are owls, eagles and hawks of coastal forests, mountains, deserts, grasslands, swamps, mangroves and offshore islands; some species are confined to specific regions or habitats, while others are extremely wide-ranging.

The diurnal birds of prey, Order Falconiformes, are divided into three families, the *Accipitridae*, the *Pandionidae*, and the *Falconidae*.

Australia's *Accipitridae* include three true eagles, the Wedge-tailed Eagle, the Australian Little Eagle and the White-breasted Sea-eagle, as well as kites (the Red-backed 'Sea-eagle' and the Whistling 'Eagle' are actually kites), goshawks and harriers. The family *Pandionidae* contains only the Osprey, a fish-catching bird of prey found around much of the Australian coastline. The third family, *Falconidae*, has six Australian species of falcon, including the Peregrine Falcon, the Little Falcon, the Kestrel and the Brown Hawk.

Nocturnal 'birds of prey', the owls, belong to the Order Strigiformes, in which there are two families—barn owls, *Tytonidae*, and typical owls, *Strigidae*.

Barn owls occur throughout Australia in suitably timbered habitats; within the group are the Barn Owl, the Masked Owl (a sub-species inhabits limestone caverns of the Nullarbor Plains and is known as the Cave Owl), the Sooty Owl and the Grass Owl. In the typical-owl family are our 'hawk-owls', the Boobook (a widespread and variable species), the Barking Owl, the Rufous Owl and the huge Powerful Owl.

The Australian Little Eagle, *Haliaetus morphnoides*, ranges almost throughout Australia except for Cape York, the south-east and Tasmania. It occurs in two distinct colour phases. The light phase is shown here; the dark phase is reddish-brown below.

Right
One of our smallest birds of prey, the Nankeen Kestrel, *Falco cenchroides*, is most often noticed hovering above grassland or open country, where it drops to the ground to capture a small reptile, rodent, spider or large insect. Here the Kestrel arrives at the nest which causes much excitement with the two young birds in the hollow.

Huge sensitive black eyes guide a Boobook Owl as it emerges from its hollow at night; the points of light in each eye are reflections of the three electronic flashes placed near the camera. When the young owls are almost ready to fly they climb to the rim of the nest hollow to await the visits of the adult birds, which begin hunting even before darkness has fully enveloped the bushland. Like other owls, the Boobook, *Ninox novaeseelandiae*, has silent flight and acute directional hearing so that it can hunt in almost total darkness. This common owl occurs throughout Australia and Tasmania in a wide variety of habitats ranging from heavy forest to semi-desert.

FAIRY WRENS

Australia's blue wrens, or fairy wrens, form a particularly colourful group; those species occurring in populated areas are among the best known of our small birds.

Although colour varies greatly, with some species having no blue at all in their plumage, the very long tails, held vertically, make these wrens easy to recognize. Many, if not all species live at times in small family groups; one nest may be attended by a pair of birds, another will have a brightly coloured male and several dull-plumaged females in attendance, while a third has two fully-plumaged males and perhaps three female or immature birds all feeding the young.

These fairy wrens, genus *Malurus*, are placed in the Old World Warbler family, *Sylviidae*, sub-family *Malurinae*. The fourteen species occupy a wide range of habitats covering most of the continent. Best known is the Blue Wren of coastal south-eastern Australia. In pairs or small parties it inhabits bushland undergrowth and is often a visitor or resident of gardens. Wrens will be seen in dry and semi-desert inland areas—the Black-backed Wren, the Blue-and-White Wren, and the Purple-backed Wren; others favour the tropical northern and north-eastern coastal strip—the Lilac-crowned Wren, the Red-backed Wren, and the Lovely Wren. Some are isolated in distant corners of the continent—the Banded or Splendid Wren, and the Red-winged Wren of south-western Australia; another, the Black-and-White Wren, occurs only on two islands off the north-western coast.

Inhabiting tropical northern and north-eastern Australia, Red-backed Wrens, *Malurus melanocephalus*, prefer tall coarse grass and thick undergrowth, often in damp places. The brownish female builds a domed nest of dead grasses close to the ground; the three or four white eggs are spotted reddish-brown.

Right
The male Red-backed Wren, ready for a takeoff, assumes a full share in feeding the young. His courtship display is spectacular, when the red is fluffed out, spreading across his back and shoulders, turning him into a living ball of fire.

4

Below left to right
The Banded Wren (or Splendid Wren),
Malurus splendens, is found in south-
western Australia. It often lives with some
other species in small family parties of
three to six birds. Occasionally two fully
plumaged males will be in the group
feeding the young at one nest.
The Blue Wren, *Malurus cyaneus*, is the
best known of the fairy wrens because its
distribution covers densely-settled south-
eastern Australia. In the dome-shaped
nest with a side entrance, placed in thick
vegetation near the ground, three or four
eggs are laid, white spotted with red
and brown.

Bottom left to right
The Variegated Wren, *Malurus lamberti*, is
one of a group of chestnut-shouldered
wrens; this species is black on the breast.
It has a wide distribution from coastal
Western Australia through the dry centre
to New South Wales and Queensland. The
nest is dome-shaped, with a side entrance;
the three eggs are white with purplish-red
markings.

A male Blue-and-white Wren, *Malurus
cyanotus*, flying across coastal heathlands.
It is distributed through arid inland areas,
reaching the coast in dry north-western
Australia.

Right
Though superficially similar to the
Variegated Wren, the Red-winged Wren,
Malurus elegans, has different colours in the
plumage, and chooses a very different
habitat. This wren inhabits swampy areas,
the dense vegetation along creeks and the
undergrowth of heavy forests; it is
confined to the extreme south-west of
Australia.

BIRDS OF SWAMPS, RIVERS & TROPICAL GRASSLANDS

Australia is one of the driest continents, so it is hardly surprising that its water birds have mainly a coastal distribution. The principal region favourable to water-bird life is the Murray–Darling river system with its many billabongs, lakes and swampy floodplains such as the Macquarie Marshes.

Most other inland waterways flow infrequently, so that their water birds must come and go with the rains, nesting where and when conditions are favourable. Many of the water-dependent birds that do inhabit the inland have developed a remarkable ability to breed very quickly after rain has filled lakes, waterholes and claypans. Among those known to nest after rain in arid parts, at any time of the year, are the Black Swan, White-faced Heron, Black Duck, Little Pied Cormorant, Black-fronted Dotterel and White-headed Stilt.

Tropical northern Australia, however, has a regular rainfall. Forty to sixty or more inches of rain may fall during the hot humid summers, flooding the extensive alluvial grassland plains and huge paperbark swamps. The water birds are then spread far and wide over the vast wet grasslands and nesting is in full swing. Among these birds of the tropical swamps and grasslands are the Brolga, the Jabiru, the Magpie Goose, Pelican, Egrets and many species of duck.

Right
Frequenting inland streams, lakes and swamps across Australia, the Darter, *Anhinga rufa*, has in common with the cormorants the habit of holding the wings out to dry after swimming. It has the ability to submerge without diving, sinking slowly until only head and neck break the surface.

Below
Magpie Geese, *Anseranus semipalmata*, occur in thousands on the swamps, billabongs and floodplains of the tropical northern coast from the Kimberleys to north-eastern Queensland.

Below left to right
A hunting White Egret, *Egretta alba*, stalks through the shallows of a swamp. This is the largest of the four or five egrets in Australia, standing almost three feet high. It nests in colonies on large platforms of sticks built in paperbark trees in a swamp; the three or four eggs are pale blue.

The Black-fronted Dotterel, *Charadrius melanops*, occurs almost throughout inland Australia on the shores of any brackish or fresh pools or swamps. The three eggs, buff-coloured and closely marked with small specks and lines, are laid in a slight hollow in sand or among stones of shore or dry river bed.

Bottom
Brolgas lift into the sky from swampy tropical grasslands where they have been feeding. The Brolga, *Grus rubicunda*, has a wide range through northern and eastern Australia, and is renowned for its dancing, which may be used in courtship display or in sheer exuberance. The Brolga is Australia's only crane except for the recently arrived Sarus Crane of Asia.

Right
The White-faced Heron, *Ardea novaehollandiae*, is a common bird of shallow coastal and inland waters, often seen hunting in flooded or moist fields and roadside ditches. The nest is a rough platform of sticks in a tall tree. It does not usually nest in colonies, although there may be several nests in close proximity. The three to five eggs are pale blue.

BIRDS OF OCEAN, SEASHORES AND LAKES

Australia's birdlife of ocean and seashore is for the most part less distinctive than its land birds; many species are summer visitors from the northern hemisphere, while others wander the oceans around the globe.

The twenty-six species of waders are migrants from Asia, as are the Pomarine Skua and the Arctic Skua. Other oceanic birds visit Australia from the south, where they breed on Antarctic and sub-Antarctic islands.

A great number of the birds of ocean and shore belong in the large Order Charadriiformes—the waders, gulls and terns. The numerous waders are divided into no less than nine families; many have two seasonal plumages, one a bright nuptial plumage, the other a dull grey-brown winter plumage, as seen when they visit Australia.

The Australian coasts are visited also by the albatrosses, petrels and shearwaters (Order Procellariiformes) which spend most of their lives at sea, coming to land only to nest. These birds have in common a tubular nostril structure and a pelargic or ocean-wandering way of life.

Penguins, too, are represented in Australian coastal waters, with Rock-hopper Penguins and Thick-billed Penguins as occasional visitors, and the Little Penguin nesting on islets of south-western and south-eastern Australia.

Below
The Silver Gull, *Larus novaehollandiae*, is the common gull of Australian shores; it occurs inland near water. The nest is a slight hollow in the ground, lined with grass or dry seaweed; the two, sometimes five, eggs are variable in colour, commonly pale greenish or brownish with dark brown markings.

Right
Found throughout Australia, both coastal and inland, the Australian Pelican, *Pelecanus conspicillatus*, feeds by probing with its long bill in shallow waters of estuaries, sheltered coasts, rivers, lakes and swamps. Pelicans breed in colonies, nesting in swamps or on islands or sand bars; the two or three eggs are dull white.

Below
Crossing a rugged coastline with powerful, graceful flight, long red tail streamers trailing behind, a Red-tailed Tropic-bird returns from the ocean to its nest on a rock ledge of a small offshore islet. This bird feeds on the open ocean, plunge-diving for small fish. It occurs on tropical and sub-tropical seas around the world, touching upon northern, north-eastern and western coasts of Australia.

Right
The Red-tailed Tropicbird, *Phaethon rubricauda*, nests on ledges on cliffs, under boulders or dense coastal scrub; the single egg is dull white with a red tinge and with reddish and brown spots and blotches. This species s a rare visitor along southern coasts of Australia.

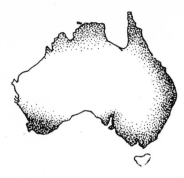

5

BIRDS OF FORESTS AND WOODLANDS

Australia's forests are principally coastal in distribution, with the greatest areas in the south-east; smaller areas occur in Tasmania and south-western Australia. Excluding the rainforests, these are of the wet sclerophyll type where rainfall is greatest, usually on coastal mountain slopes, or of the dry sclerophyll type; eucalypts are dominant and often the only large trees.

Woodlands cover a far greater area. There are extensive tracts of grassland with scattered trees across tropical northern Australia and north-eastern Australia, and there are woodland areas in the south-east and south-west, generally inland of the more heavily timbered coastal ranges.

These forests and woodlands are the home of a great variety of birds, which exploit every level. In the treetop foliage will be seen the Red-tipped, Red-browed and Spotted Pardalotes; on the treetrunks and branches are Rufous Tree-creepers, Shrike-tits and various Sittellas which search for insects in crevices of the bark. Open clearings are favoured by Rainbow Birds, Tree Martins and other birds which take insects in the air. Other birds, including the Sacred Kingfisher, capture their prey on the forest floor by dropping suddenly from a perch in the trees.

Many forest birds, like the Golden Whistler, Mistletoe Bird, Spotted Pardalote and Sacred Kingfisher have a wide range, being found from north-eastern to south-western Australia, while some, including the Western Shrike-tit, are restricted to forests or woodlands of one particular region.

Below
Australia has nine species of treecreepers. They search the crevices of the bark for small insects, beginning at the base of the trunk and spiralling upwards with quick jerky movements, then from the top of the tree gliding to the base of the next tree to begin another search. This Rufous Treecreeper, *Climacteris rufa*, is a species confined to south-western Australia; the nest is built in a hollow limb.
Right
The Olive-backed Oriole, *Oriolus sagittatus*, inhabits the forests and woodlands of northern, eastern and south-eastern Australia, where it feeds on native berries and fruits, and insects. The nest is woven among twigs of the outer foliage at any height up to sixty feet above the ground; the two to four eggs are pale cream with brown and grey markings.

Below left to right
A Tree Martin, *Hylochelidon nigricans*, flies to its nest in a small hollow; martins spend most of their time circling and diving through the air in pursuit of flying insects. The Tree Martin is found throughout Australia and Tasmania, though less common in the northern and very dry central regions.

Bottom left to right
A male Spotted Pardalote, *Pardalotus punctatus*, carries strips of bark into the tunnel which has its entrance between the boulders; he is building a globular nest in a chamber at the end of the tunnel.
As the Spotted Pardalote dives into the entrance of his nest tunnel the rows of white spots for which he is named are clearly visible. Pardalotes frequent the treetop foliage, where they find small insects on leaves and foliage.
The female pardalote takes her turn to feed the young. Spotted Pardalotes occur in eastern, south-eastern and south-western Australia, and in Tasmania.

Right
With legs outstretched to cushion the impact of landing, a little Striated Pardalote, *Pardalotus substriatus*, lands at the small knot-hole in which its domed nest of bark is built. One of seven or eight species, the Striated Pardalote is widespread throughout southern Australia wherever there is forest or woodland habitat. The pardalotes are birds of the treetops, where they feed upon small insects on the foliage.

Below
A male Mistletoe Bird, *Dicaeum hirundinaceum*, with beak full of sticky mistletoe seeds taken from the fruits of the mistletoe on which he is perched. He skilfully nips the centre of the ripe yellow berry and takes out the seed which is covered with a thick white sticky sweet layer; these seeds are then swallowed whole or carried to the nest.

Bottom
With wings half closed the Mistletoe Bird swoops up to the nest with mistletoe seeds for the young birds. The nest is a soft, suspended pear-shaped structure with a vertical slit entrance in one side. Mistletoe Birds are considered to be largely responsible for spreading the parasitic mistletoe plants from tree to tree; they occur throughout Australia wherever trees and mistletoes grow.

6

Left
A Western Warbler, *Gerygone fusca*, returning to its small globular nest suspended from the twigs of a lakeside tree.
Right
The rich and powerful calls of the Golden Whistler, *Pachycephala pectoralis*, are among the commonest sounds in Australian coastal forests during spring, when rival male whistlers establish and defend their nesting territories. The male Golden Whistler here is flying down to land beside the relatively dull-plumaged female.
Below
The Sacred Kingfisher, *Halcyon sancta*, inhabits woodlands, open clearings in forests, mangroves and tree-lined watercourses of the interior. It preys upon small reptiles, frogs and large insects and nests in a hollow of a tree, or a tunnel drilled into a termite nest or creek bank.

Below left to right
The Red-browed Pardalote, *Pardalotus rubricatus*, occurs across tropical northern Australia. In a chamber at the end of a two-foot tunnel excavated by the birds a domed nest of bark strips is constructed, and three or four white eggs laid.

The largest of the kingfisher family, the Laughing Kookaburra, *Dacelo gigas*, is one of Australia's best-known birds. Although it may occasionally kill a small snake, its prey more often consists of small lizards, small mammals, and fledgling birds taken from their nests. Formerly confined to eastern and south-eastern Australia, the Kookaburra has been introduced into Western Australia and Tasmania.

Bottom left to right
The Black-faced Wood-Swallow, *Artamus cinereus*, commonly builds a cup-shaped nest in a stump or branch with a slight hollow. It is a bird of open woodlands of the interior and sub-interior, reaching the coast in the north and west. The four eggs are white, spotted with brown and blue-grey.

This Western Shriketit, *Falcunculus leucogaster*, is found in woodland country in south-western Australia. It builds a neat, deep, cup-shaped nest, closely matted with cobwebs and usually high in the top of a tall eucalypt.

Laughing Kookaburra *Dacelo gigas*
RANGE north-eastern to south-eastern
Australia; introduced to W.A., Tas.
HABITAT open forest country.
COLOUR upper parts and wings brown, with
patches of blue and white on wings; head
light brown, underparts white.
LENGTH 16–18 in.

1 EMUS & CASSOWARIES Order: Casuariiformes
  Cassowaries: Family *Casuariidae*
  Emus: Family *Dromiceidae*

2 GREBE-LIKE BIRDS Order: Podicepediformes
  Grebes: Family *Podicepedidae*

3 TUBE-NOSED SWIMMERS Order: Procellariiformes
  Albatrosses: Family *Diomedeidae*
  Petrels & Mutton-birds: Family *Procellariidae*
  Storm-Petrels: Family *Hydrobatidae*

4 PENGUINS Order: Sphenisciformes
  Penguins: Family *Spheniscidae*

5 PELICANS, etc. Order: Pelecaniformes
  Tropic-birds: Family *Phaethontidae*
  Pelicans: Family *Pelecanidae*
  Gannets & Boobies: Family *Sulidae*
  Cormorants: Family *Phalacrocoracidae*
  Darters or Snakebirds: Family *Anhingidae*
  Frigate-birds: Family *Fregatidae*

6 HERON-LIKE BIRDS Order: Ciconiiformes
  Herons, Egrets & Bitterns: Family *Ardeidae*
  Storks & Jabirus: Family *Ciconiidae*
  Ibises & Spoonbills: Family *Threskiornithidae*

7 WATERFOWL Order: Anseriformes
  Swans, Geese & Ducks: Family *Anatidae*

8 DIURNAL BIRDS OF PREY Order: Falconiformes
  Eagles, Goshawks, etc.: Family *Accipitridae*
  Ospreys: Family *Pandionidae*
  Falcons & Kestrels: Family *Falconidae*

9 FOWL-LIKE BIRDS Order: Galliformes
  Mound-builders: Family *Megapodiidae*
  Pheasants & Quails: Family *Phasianidae*

10 CRANES, RAILS, etc. Order: Gruiformes
  Bustard Quails: Family *Turnicidae*
  Cranes: Family *Gruidae*
  Rails, Crakes & Water-hens: Family *Rallidae*
  Bustards: Family *Otidae*

11 WADERS, GULLS & TERNS Order: Charadriiformes
  Lilly-trotters: Family *Jacanidae*
  Painted Snipes: Family *Rostratulidae*
  Oystercatchers: Family *Haematopodidae*
  Plovers & Dotterels: Family *Charadriidae*
  Curlews, Sandpipers & Snipes: Family *Scolopacidae*
  Stilts & Avocets: Family *Recurvirostridae*
  Stone-Curlews: Family *Burhinidae*
  Pratincoles & Coursers: Family *Glareolidae*
  Gulls & Terns: Family *Laridae*
  Skuas: Family *Stercorariidae*

12 PIGEONS & DOVES Order: Columbiformes
  Pigeons & Doves: Family *Columbidae*

13 PARROTS & COCKATOOS Order: Psittaciformes
  Parrots, Cockatoos, Lorikeets, etc.: Family *Psittacidae*

14 CUCKOO-LIKE BIRDS Order: Cuculiformes
  Cuckoos: Family *Cuculidae*

15 OWLS Order: Strigiformes
  Hawk-Owls: Family *Strigidae*
  Barn-Owls: Family *Tytonidae*

16 FROGMOUTHS & NIGHTJARS Order: Caprimulgiformes
  Frogmouths: Family *Podargidae*
  Owlet-Nightjars: Family *Aegothelidae*
  Nightjars: Family *Caprimulgidae*

17 SWIFTS Order: Apodiformes
  Swifts: Family *Apodidae*

18 KINGFISHERS & ALLIED BIRDS Order: Coraciformes
  Kingfishers: Family *Alcedinidae*
  Bee-eaters: Family *Meropidae*
  Rollers: Family *Coraciidae*

19 PERCHING or SONG-BIRDS Order: Passeriformes
  Pittas: Family *Pittidae*
  Lyrebirds: Family *Menuridae*
  Scrub-birds: Family *Atrichornithidae*
  Larks: Family *Alaudidae*
  Swallows & Martins: Family *Hirundinidae*
  Cuckoo-shrikes, Trillers & Cicada-birds: Family *Campephagidae*
  Drongos: Family *Dicruridae*
  Orioles & Figbirds: Family *Oriolidae*
  Crows & allied birds: Family *Corvidae*
  Mudlarks, Choughs & Apostle-birds: Family *Grallinidae*
  Magpies, Butcher-birds & Currawongs: Family *Cracticidae*

Bower-birds & Cat-birds: Family *Ptilonorhynchidae*
Birds of Paradise & Manucode: Family *Paradisaeidae*
Australian Treecreepers: Family *Climacteridae*
Nuthatches & related birds: Family *Sittidae*
Babblers, Quail-Thrushes & Log-runners: Family *Timaliidae*
Thrushes: Family *Turdidae*
Old World Warblers: Family *Sylviidae*
Old World Flycatchers: Family *Muscicapidae*
Pipits: Family *Motacillidae*
Wood-Swallows: Family *Artamidae*
Honeyeaters: Family *Meliphagidae*
Shriketits, Crested Bellbird, Wedgebill & Whipbirds: Family *Falcunculidae*
Chats: Family *Epthianuridae*
Sunbirds: Family *Nectariniidae*
Mistletoe-Bird & Pardalotes: Family *Dicaeidae*
Silvereyes: Family *Zosteropidae*
Old World Seedeaters: Family *Ploceidae*

Shy Albatross *Diomeda cauta*
Range: seas around southern Australia, breeding on Albatross Island in Bass Strait.
Colour: white, with black on upper wings and mantle; tips of the under wings black.
Length: 40 in. Wingspan 8 ft.

Little Egret *Egretta garzetta*
Range: northern and eastern Australia.
Habitat: swamps, streams, lake shores.
Colour: pure white (with plumes on back in breeding season); legs black, beak black.
Length: 22 in.

Black-shouldered Kite *Elanus notatus*
Range: throughout coastal Australia, at times well inland.
Habitat: open, lightly timbered country, paddocks, grassland areas.
Colour: upper parts light grey, black on shoulders, dark flight quills; undersurfaces white.
Length: 13–14 in. Wingspan 33–37 in.

BIRD FAMILIES

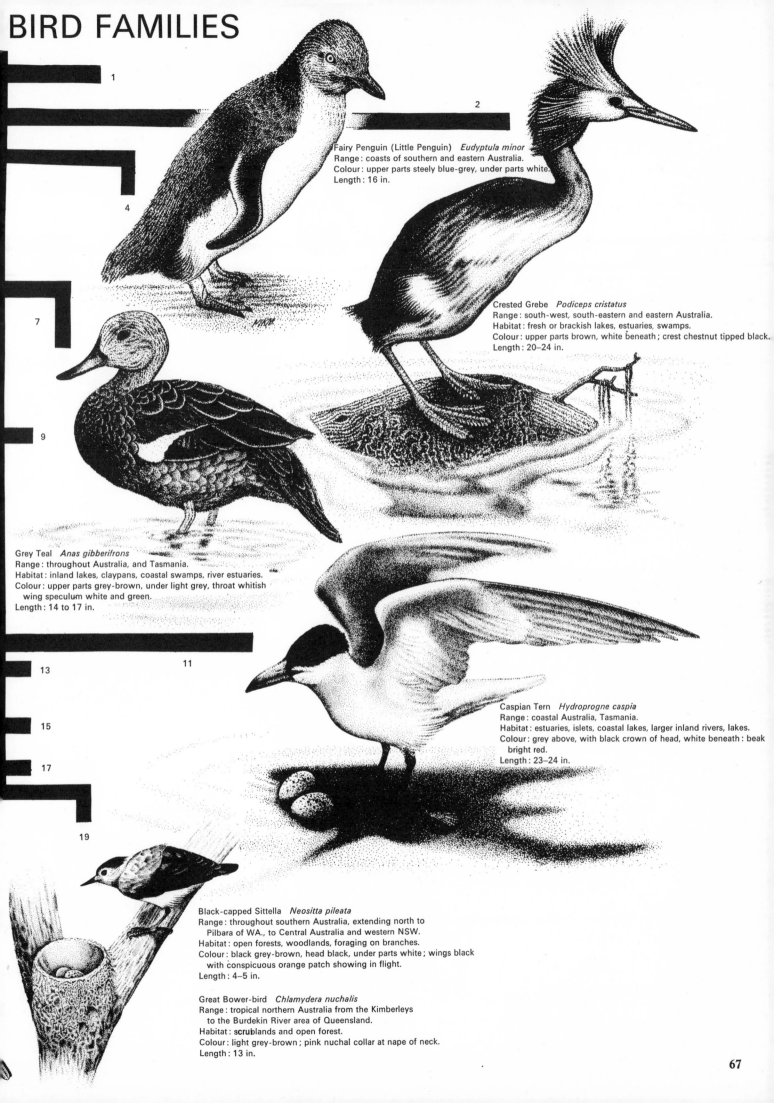

1

2

Fairy Penguin (Little Penguin) *Eudyptula minor*
Range: coasts of southern and eastern Australia.
Colour: upper parts steely blue-grey, under parts white.
Length: 16 in.

4

Crested Grebe *Podiceps cristatus*
Range: south-west, south-eastern and eastern Australia.
Habitat: fresh or brackish lakes, estuaries, swamps.
Colour: upper parts brown, white beneath; crest chestnut tipped black.
Length: 20–24 in.

7

9

Grey Teal *Anas gibberifrons*
Range: throughout Australia, and Tasmania.
Habitat: inland lakes, claypans, coastal swamps, river estuaries.
Colour: upper parts grey-brown, under light grey, throat whitish
wing speculum white and green.
Length: 14 to 17 in.

13

11

15

Caspian Tern *Hydroprogne caspia*
Range: coastal Australia, Tasmania.
Habitat: estuaries, islets, coastal lakes, larger inland rivers, lakes.
Colour: grey above, with black crown of head, white beneath: beak
bright red.
Length: 23–24 in.

17

19

Black-capped Sittella *Neositta pileata*
Range: throughout southern Australia, extending north to
Pilbara of WA., to Central Australia and western NSW.
Habitat: open forests, woodlands, foraging on branches.
Colour: black grey-brown, head black, under parts white; wings black
with conspicuous orange patch showing in flight.
Length: 4–5 in.

Great Bower-bird *Chlamydera nuchalis*
Range: tropical northern Australia from the Kimberleys
to the Burdekin River area of Queensland.
Habitat: scrublands and open forest.
Colour: light grey-brown; pink nuchal collar at nape of neck.
Length: 13 in.

TECHNIQUES FOR BIRD PHOTOGRAPHY

The major difficulty to be overcome when photographing birds wild and free in their natural bushland habitat is their very strong fear of man and his devices. Their shyness can be overcome in two ways—partly by the choice of the correct photographic equipment, and secondly by the employment oi techniques designed either to ensure that the bird is not aware of the presence of photographer and camera, or that the bird is so gradually introduced to the photographic equipment that it will accept it without abandoning the nest.

For most amateur bird photographers one of the many 35 mm single lens reflex cameras will be the most suitable choice; it is important that the camera has a quiet shutter, and that a long telephoto lens is available for it.

For those who prefer a larger format, there are single lens reflex, monorail and press-type cameras which provide the necessary accurate ground-glass focussing and viewing, and give pictures of $2\frac{1}{4} \times 2\frac{1}{4}$ inches, $2\frac{1}{4} \times 3\frac{1}{4}$, or larger. The photographs in this book, with the exception of one or two on 35 mm, were taken with Plaubel Profia monorail camera, Mamiya R B 67 single lens reflex, or Bronica S.L.R. fitted with 400 mm telephoto lens. The film used was Ektachrome Professional and Agfacolor CT 18 rollfilm.

Because wild birds are so wary a close approach is generally not possible except at the nest, where their strong parental instincts will make them return remarkably close to camera and flash equipment. When working at nests it is most important to proceed slowly, and to abandon all attempts at photography if the birds seem very reluctant to return, otherwise desertion of the nest and death of the young will be almost certain consequences.

Nests of the small colourful songbirds such as fairy wrens and robins are generally very well concealed or camouflaged. Rather than search for the nest itself it is better to follow the adult birds at a distance, watching through binoculars for signs of food or nesting material being carried in their beaks.

Small birds may be photographed either from a hide, or by using a remote control shutter release. The hide, a simple box-like framework covered with canvas or hessian, must be erected first some distance from the nest, and brought closer over a period of a day or so. It is vital that the covering be secured tightly, so that it will not flap in the wind and frighten the birds from their nest in the photographer's absence. The camera is trained upon the nest through a slit in the front of the hide.

Instead of a hide close to the nest, it is possible to place the camera on a tripod near the nest, and operate the shutter by means of a remote control device. This may be simply a rubber bulb connected by twenty or thirty feet of thin plastic tube to a plunger screwed into the camera's cable release socket, triggering the shutter by air pressure. This device has the disadvantage of a significant time delay.

Others operate electrically, by means of a small solenoid to trigger the camera, and wires leading to battery and switch forty or fifty feet away. In the case of flight photographs a light beam device can be used to actuate the solenoid, triggering the solenoid (and simultaneously the electronic flash) the instant the flying bird's shadow falls upon the transistorized photoelectric receiving unit.

When working with remote control equipment it is essential that the camera be set up on its tripod some distance from the nest, then brought closer over a period of an hour or so, making sure that the parent birds succeed in feeding the young after each shift of the camera towards the nest.

Larger birds in most cases must be photographed from a hide. Such nests are usually in trees, involving a great deal more work in building a platform and hide among the branches. For lower nests, up to about twenty-five feet, a tower of slotted angle steel may be constructed, while others at heights up to eighty feet are photographed by building on the branches. If there are no limbs in a suitable position for a hide it may not be possible to photograph the bird.

Work must be done a little at a time, over a period of days or weeks. In the case of eagles, hawks, parrots and some other birds it is often necessary to arrange that two people walk or climb to the completed hide, then after the equipment is set up the photographer remains in the hide while the other person departs. With luck the bird soon returns, thinking that both have gone.

Most nests are situated in undergrowth, beneath tree foliage or other natural cover which causes lighting difficulties: either it is too dark in the shade, or there is a confused dappled effect of sunlight through foliage. It is therefore usual to employ flash for lighting. For 'stills' of birds perched or sitting on the nest, flashbulbs or a small inexpensive electronic flash will be satisfactory, but for flight photographs, particularly of small birds whose wings beat extremely rapidly, a high-speed flash unit is essential.

Most electronic flash units emit a burst of light lasting 1/1000 to 1/2000th of a second, which is not brief enough to 'freeze' small birds in flight. There are very few units sufficiently fast; I am at present using a Multiblitz 111b which gives 1/3000th second with one flash head plugged in, 1/5000 with two heads, and 1/7000 with three as used for most of the photos in this book.

A further complication arises if natural sunlight is combined with flash, as the camera shutter is comparatively slow at its fastest, 1/500th second. It is necessary that there be no sunlight on the flying bird (it must be in shade of bush or tree) so that it will be illuminated by flash only. The distant natural background, however, will not be reached by the flash, so must be exposed by natural light, usually direct sunlight.

A balance (between sunlight on background and flash on bird) must be set by selecting first the shutter speed, then a lens aperture to correctly expose the sunlit background, and finally, the three flash heads are fixed at a distance from the bird to give correct exposure of the bird at the aperture already selected for correct background exposure.

Because the background is exposed by sunlight at the relatively slow 1/500th or 1/250th of the shutter, and the bird

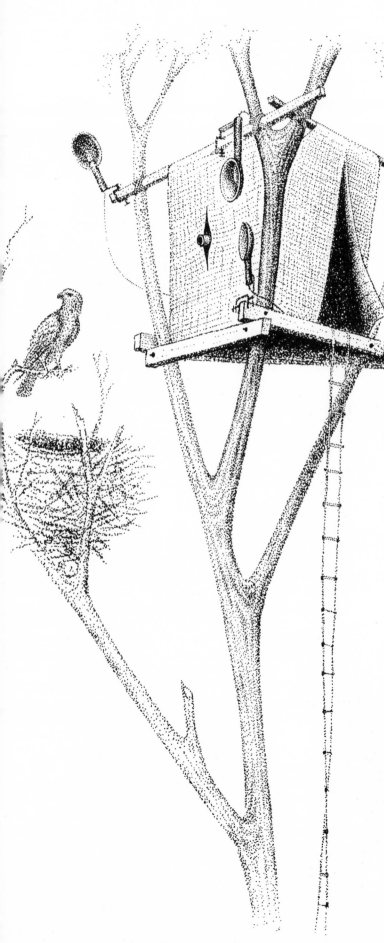

itself by the 1/7000th of the flash, a flying bird taken by this synchro-sun technique may be edged with a dark blurred outline, particularly where fast-moving wingtips are seen against the sky. The plumage details are still sharply rendered, while the slight dark edge blur gives a greater feeling of movement to the picture.

For photos in this book, hides have been built in trees at heights up to 80 feet, although more usually 30 to 50 feet above ground.

This treetop hide at a hawk's nest, shows the hide construction, a wire rope ladder, electronic flashes in position, and camera lens protruding.

ACKNOWLEDGMENTS

During the years since 1959, when the first of the photographs in this book were taken, I have been given assistance by many people. The preparations involved for bird photography can be lengthy, and quite difficult if a hide must be built in treetops at heights up to eighty feet, when there may be some small element of danger. It is on such occasions that the help of several very enthusiastic amateur bird photographers has been greatly appreciated. To these, and to all others who have helped by finding nests or giving useful information or assisting in any way in the preliminary work involved, I wish to make known my sincere thanks. Among those closely involved over the years were Ian Edgar (Ardross, WA.), Malcom Lewis (Armadale, WA.), Roly Paine (Gibraltar Range National Park, NSW.), John Courtney (Glen Innes, NSW.), Ray Garstone (Woodanilling, WA.), Mary and Jim Hargreaves (Armadale, WA.), Pat and Peter Slater (Brisbane, Qld.), Roy Stirling (Atherton, Qld.), Frank and Gwen Bailey (Manypeaks, WA.), Betty and Wal McKenzie (Brisbane, Qld.), Phil Fuller (South Perth, WA.), Elva and Jim Watson (Balwyn, Vic.), Neville Fenton (Dorrigo, NSW.), Arthur Stafford (Dorrigo, NSW.).

Bird photography involves travel to remote areas, long absences and inconvenient hours of work; for her tolerance and understanding during the years of bird photography I would like to record my special thanks to my wife Irene.

M.M.

BIRDS OF THE ADELAIDE - MELBOURNE-

Crested Grebe, lakes, streams, swamps
Hoary-headed Grebe, lakes and swamps
Fairy Penguin, coast and islands
Yellow-billed Spoonbill, swamps and lakes
Chestnut-breasted Shelduck, lakes and swamps
Musk Duck, lakes and coastal inlets
Hooded Dotterel, seashores and coastal lagoons
Short-tailed Shearwater, breeds on southern islands
Fairy Prion, southern seas and islands
Sooty Oyster-catcher, rocky shores and reefs
White-capped Albatross, southern seas
Cape Barren Goose, grasslands and swampy fields
Plumed Egret, swamps, lakes and streams
Collared Sparrowhawk, open forest
Grey Goshawk, forests
Swamp Harrier, swamps and reedbeds
Swamp Quail, swampy grasslands
Painted Quail, open forest and heathlands
Spotted Crake, marshes and reeds
Spotless Crake, swamps and reeds
Marsh Crake, swamps and reeds
Tasmanian Native Hen, marshes and reedbeds
Green Rosella, forests and clearings
Orange-breasted Parrot, grasslands and open forest
Swift Parrot, flowering eucalypts
Musk Lorikeet, flowering gums
Purple-crowned Lorikeet, flowering eucalypts
Little Lorikeet, flowering eucalypts
Yellow-tailed Black Cockatoo, forests
Gang Gang Cockatoo, forested ranges
Crimson Rosella, forests and ranges
Tasmanian Masked Owl, forests
Powerful Owl, mountain forests
Tawny Frogmouth, forests
Spine-tailed Swift, open skies
Laughing Kookaburra, open forest
Superb Lyrebird, dense forest
Clinking Currawong, Tasmanian lowlands
Reed-warbler, reedbeds
Blue Wren, forests and thickets
Southern Emu-wren, swampy heathlands
Yellow-throated Scrub-wren, rainforest
Pink Robin, heavily timbered ranges
Rose Robin, coastal rainforest
Southern Yellow Robin, forests
Grey Fantail, forests
Rufous Fantail, summer visitor, dense forest
Black-faced Flycatcher, forests
Eastern Spinebill, heaths and open forest
Fuscous Honeyeater, open forest
Helmeted Honeyeater, forests
New Holland Honeyeater, heathlands
Bell-miner, forests
Spotted Pardalote, foliage, open and heavy forest

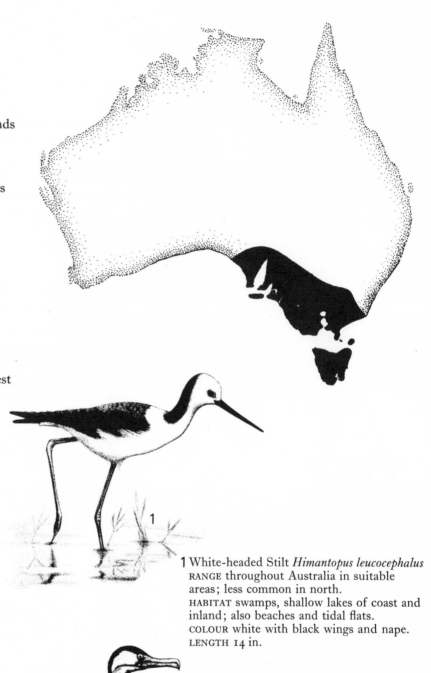

1 White-headed Stilt *Himantopus leucocephalus*
RANGE throughout Australia in suitable
areas; less common in north.
HABITAT swamps, shallow lakes of coast and
inland; also beaches and tidal flats.
COLOUR white with black wings and nape.
LENGTH 14 in.

2 Pied Cormorant *Phalacrocorax varius*
RANGE coastal Australia and Tas., extending
to suitable inland localities.
HABITAT swamps, lakes, streams, inlets,
rocky islets.
COLOUR black above, white below.
LENGTH (male) 31–32 in.; (female) 27–29 in.

HOBART REGION

3 Superb Lyrebird *Menura superba*
RANGE coastal eastern Australia, from south-east Qld. to vicinity of Melbourne.
HABITAT rainforest, wet sclerophyll forest.
COLOUR brown above, grey beneath.
LENGTH 27 in.

4 Sharp-tailed Sandpiper *Erolia acuminata*
RANGE a migrant visitor to Australia (from Siberia).
HABITAT margins of salt-marshes, sand-flats of inlets, rivers; also inland swamps, lakes.
COLOUR upper streaked brown, grey, and black, crown of head rufous and black; underparts buff and brown, with throat and abdomen white.
LENGTH males 9 in., females 7 in.

5 Hooded Dotterel *Charadrius cucullatus*
RANGE southern coasts of Australia and Tas.
HABITAT sea coasts, estuaries and inland salt lakes.
COLOUR upper parts brown; head, throat very dark brown; underparts white.
LENGTH $7\frac{1}{2}$ in.

6 Yellow-billed Spoonbill *Platalea flavipes*
RANGE most of Australia (except the centre), Cape York and Tas.
HABITAT swamps, wet flats, margins of lakes, rivers.
COLOUR white, beak and legs yellow; bluish bare face skin.
LENGTH 3 ft. wingspan 5 ft.

7 Black Duck *Anas superciliosa*
RANGE throughout Australia (except the desert areas) and Tas.
HABITAT mainly freshwater swamps, lakes, pools, but also tidal flats, estuaries.
COLOUR upper parts dark brown, throat white, undersurface brown, white-striped head, green wing speculum.
LENGTH 19–22 in.

BIRDS OF THE CANBERRA - SYDNEY -

Glossy Ibis, swamps and grasslands
Plumed Tree-duck, lakes and swamps
Little Eagle, inland plains and open forest
Black-shouldered Kite, open and light-timbered forest
Collared Sparrowhawk, open forest
Grey Goshawk, forests
Peregrine Falcon, forests and mountains
Little Falcon, forests, timbered ranges
Kestrel, open forest, paddocks and plains
Brush Turkey, rainforests and scrubs
King Quail, swampy grasslands, nomadic
Brolga, plains and swamps
Jacana, lagoons and swamps
Wonga Pigeon, rainforest
Green-winged Pigeon, rainforest
Rainbow Lorikeet, eucalypt forests
Scaly-breasted Lorikeet, open forest
Glossy Black Cockatoo, forests
Pink, or Major Mitchell Cockatoo, mallee and semi-arid areas
Sulphur-crested Cockatoo, forests
Galah, open forests and plains
Cockatiel, inland plains and scrubs
Superb Parrot, open forest and grasslands
King Parrot, dense forests
Paradise Parrot, grasslands
Regent Parrot, mallee and open forest
Yellow Rosella, grassland and open forest
Eastern Rosella, open forest
Red-backed Parrot, grasslands
Blue bonnet, grasslands and open scrub
Turquoise Parrot, grasslands and open forest
Scarlet-chested Parrot, dry interior, rare
Brush Cuckoo, rainforest
Masked Owl, forest
Boobook Owl, forest
Spotted Owl, dense forests
Azure Kingfisher, fresh and saltwater streams
Mangrove Kingfisher, mangroves
Sacred Kingfisher, forests
Forest Kingfisher, woodlands and forests
Rainbow Bird, coastal forests to inland plains
Dollar-bird, forests and jungle
Buff-breasted Pitta, rainforest
Prince Albert Lyrebird, rainforest
Rufous Scrub-bird, rainforest
Southern Figbird, jungle and open forest
Pied Currawong, forests
Regent Bower-bird, rainforests
Satin Bower-bird, rainforests
Spotted Bower-bird, inland scrub
Green Catbird, rainforest
Brown Tree-creeper, open forest
White-headed Sittella, open forest
Chestnut-crowned Babbler, inland scrub
Cinnamon Quail-thrush, arid, stony country
Rufous Songlark, open areas

Tailor-bird, swampy areas
Tawny Grass-bird, reedbeds
Red-backed Wren, creekside grasses and undergrowth
Chestnut-tailed Heath-wren, heaths
Inland Thornbill, thickets and low scrub
Shy Ground-wren, mallee scrub
Rock-warbler, ravines and hillsides near streams
Red-capped Robin, inland forest, scrub
Hooded Robin, forest and scrub
Northern Yellow Robin, rainforest
Rufous Fantail, rainforest
Golden Whistler, jungle and forest
Olive Whistler, rainforest
Rufous Whistler, open forest
Restless Flycatcher, open forest
Black-faced Wood-swallow, open country
Painted Honeyeater, forests
Yellow-plumed Honeyeater, mallee
Blue-faced Honeyeater, open forest
Scarlet Honeyeater, flowering trees, nomadic
Regent Honeyeater, nomadic
Lewin Honeyeater, rainforests
New Holland Honeyeater, coastal heathlands
Noisy Friar-bird, nomadic
Eastern Shrike-tit, open forest
Eastern Whip-bird, rainforest and thickets
Beautiful Firetail, heath and low scrub
Chestnut-breasted Finch, reedbeds and grasslands
Plum-headed Finch, open country

BRISBANE REGION

1 Brush Turkey *Alectura lathami*
RANGE coastal north-eastern Australia, Cape York to vicinity of Sydney.
HABITAT rainforests and dense scrubs.
COLOUR body black, head and neck red, with a yellow 'collar'.

2 Nankeen Night-Heron *Nycticorax caledonicus*
RANGE most of mainland Australia and Tas.
HABITAT swamps, river banks.
COLOUR upper parts bright brown, undersurface white, head black.
LENGTH 21–25 in.

3 Peregrine Falcon *Falco peregrinus*
RANGE mainland Australia (except the centre) and Tas.
HABITAT mountainous or heavily timbered country.
COLOUR upper parts slate blue-grey; head, neck, cheeks and wings black; breast chestnut; abdomen chestnut spotted black; flanks, thighs and under wing coverts light chestnut finely barred with black.
LENGTH male 15 in., wingspan 32 in.; female length 18½ in.

4 Collared Sparrowhawk *Accipiter cirrocephalus*
RANGE mainland Australia and Tas.
HABITAT open and lightly-timbered country.
COLOUR upper parts dark slaty-grey, with reddish-brown collar; undersurface rufous brown with narrow white cross-bars.
LENGTH (female) 14–15 in., wingspan 2 ft. 6 in.; length (male) 12 in.

5 Royal Spoonbill *Platalea regia*

6 Brolgas (display dance) *Grus rubicunda*
RANGE throughout Australia except the south-west and coastal south-east.
HABITAT plains, grasslands and open swampy areas.
COLOUR silvery-grey, wings dark brown, red skin on sides of face, back of neck.
LENGTH 40–50 in. wingspan 7 ft.

7 Banded Plover *Zonifer tricolor*
RANGE mainland Australia (rare in far north) and Tas.
HABITAT grasslands and plains.
COLOUR upper parts brown, head black with white eye streak; undersurface white with black chest band; red wattle between eye and beak.
LENGTH 10 in.

BIRDS OF BROOME-DARWIN-TOWNSVILLE

Cassowary, Cape York rainforest
Jabiru, swamps and lagoons
Green Pygmy Goose, swamps and mangroves
Pied, or Magpie Goose, swamps and mangroves
White-breasted Sea Eagle, coast and rivers
Crested Hawk, forests, and riverbank trees
Red Goshawk, open forests
Jungle Fowl, rainforest
White-quilled Rock Pigeon, spinifex sandstone
Chestnut-quilled Rock Pigeon, sandstone hills
Rose-crowned Pigeon, coastal rainforest
Wompoo Pigeon, rainforest
Torres Strait Pigeon, rainforest
Northern Rosella, open forests
Red-collared Lorikeet, open forests
Cloncurry Parrot, grassland and river trees
Crimson-winged Parrot, open forest and river trees
Varied Lorikeet, open forests, riverbank trees
Red-browed Fig Parrot, rainforest
Great Palm Cockatoo, jungle and open forest
Eclectus, or Red-sided Parrot, rainforest
Hooded Parrot, open forest and spinifex
Golden-shouldered Parrot, open forest
Northern Boobook, jungle and open forest
Rufous Owl, open forest
Papuan Frogmouth, jungle and open forest
Little Kingfisher, rainforest and mangroves
Yellow-billed Kingfisher, jungle and open forest
White-tailed Kingfisher, rainforest
Blue-breasted Pitta, rainforest
Papuan Cuckoo-shrike, open forest and mangroves
Spangled Drongo, jungle and open forest
Yellow Oriole, open forest
Olive-backed Oriole, jungle and open forest
Shining Starling, rainforest
Yellow Fig-bird, forests
Golden Bower-bird, rainforests above 3,000 feet
Tooth-billed Cat (or Bower) Bird, rainforest
Prince Albert Rifle-bird, rainforest
Queen Victoria Rifle-bird, rainforest
Manucode, rainforest
Black-headed Log-runner, rainforest
Northern Scrub-robin, rainforest
Purple-backed Wren, low scrub and spinifex
Lovely Wren, low scrub and spinifex
Lilac-crowned Wren, cane-grass and pandanus
Fern-wren, rainforest
Lemon-breasted Flycatcher, forests
Little Yellow Robin, in and near rainforests
Pale Yellow Robin, rainforest
Buff-sided Robin, rainforest and mangroves
Pearly Flycatcher, jungle and open forest
Spectacled Flycatcher, rainforest
Brown-tailed Flycatcher, open forest and mangrove
Leaden Flycatcher, coastal forests

Broad-billed Flycatcher, mangroves
Pied Flycatcher, rainforest
Frill-necked Flycatcher, rainforest
Golden-backed Honeyeater, open woodland
Red-headed Honeyeater, mangrove and forest
Yellow-breasted Sunbird, rainforest fringes and clearings
Black-headed Pardalote, woodland and riverbanks
Red-browed Pardalote, woodland and riverbanks
Crimson Finch, grasslands and pandanus
Gouldian Finch, grasslands and spinifex
Painted Finch, grasslands and spinifex
Masked Finch, grasslands
Pictorella Finch, grasslands
Yellow-tailed Finch, cane-grass swamps
Long-tailed Finch, grasslands

Plumed Egret *Egretta intermedia*
RANGE northern, eastern and south-eastern
Australia.
HABITAT swamps, margins of lakes, streams.
COLOUR pure white, with beak yellow, legs
black below, yellow above knees.
LENGTH 24 in.

REGION

1 White Ibis *Threskiornis molucca*

2 Great Palm Cockatoo *Probosciger aterrimus*
RANGE Cape York Peninsula, Qld.; also
New Guinea.
HABITAT rainforest, venturing into nearby
savannah woodlands to feed.
COLOUR grey-black above and below, naked
cheek-patches crimson.
LENGTH 25 in.

3 Jabiru *Xenorhynchus asiaticus*
RANGE northern and eastern Australia.
HABITAT swamps, lagoons, saltwater creeks
and tidal flats.
COLOUR body white, head and neck dark
metallic green, wings brown, tail green,
legs red.
LENGTH 4–4½ ft. wingspan 6½–7 ft.

4 Greater Frigate-bird *Fregata minor*
RANGE seas of northern and north-eastern
Australia, occasionally venturing to
southern seas.
HABITAT the tropical oceans.
COLOUR almost black, except for the red
distensible neck pouch.
LENGTH 34–40 in.

5 Plumed Tree-duck *Dendrocygna eytoni*

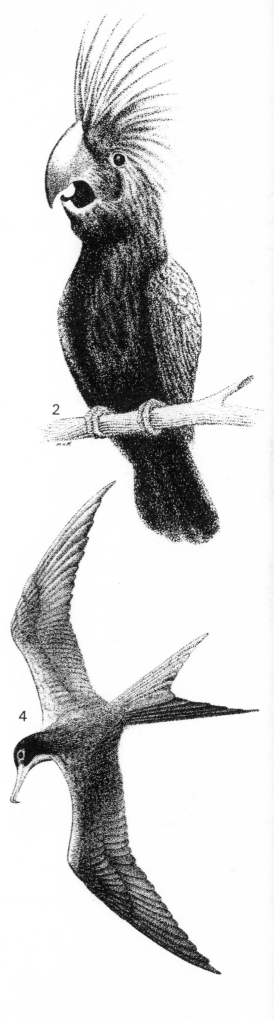

BIRDS OF THE PERTH REGION

Emu, plains and open forests
Nankeen Night Heron, streams and swamps
Mangrove Bittern, muddy foreshores
Red Mangrove Bittern, coastal area, Onslow district
Black Swan, lakes, rivers and swamps
Whistling Eagle, plains and open forest
Fork-tailed Kite, inland plains
Letter-wing Kite, open and lightly-timbered land
Brown Goshawk, forests
Spotted Harrier, swamps and reedbeds
Brown Hawk, open country
Banded Rail, swampy areas
Black-tailed Native Hen, swamps and reedbeds
Western Swamphen, lakes and streams
Bustard, inland plains
Red-capped Dotterel, beaches, lakes
Black-fronted Dotterel, river banks
Crested Pigeon, inland scrubs
Flock Pigeon, plains
Western Plumed Pigeon, rocky and spinifex
Red-tailed Black Cockatoo, forests
Mulga Parrot, open forest and dry scrub
Bourke Parrot, mulga scrubs
Long-billed Corella, inland plains
Western Rosella, open forest
Twenty-eight Parrot, open forest
Red-capped Parrot, south-west forests
Elegant Grass Parrot, plains and grasslands
Rock Parrot, islands and south coast
Swamp Parrot, swampy heathlands
Tawny Frogmouth, forests
Owlet Nightjar, forests
Mangrove Kingfisher, mangrove swamps
Red-backed Kingfisher, dry interior
Blue-winged Kookaburra, open forests, and mangroves
Ground Cuckoo-shrike, mallee and mulga
Noisy Scrub-bird, low coastal thickets
White-backed Swallow, inland areas
Western Magpie, open forest
Rufous Tree-creeper, open forest
Western Bower-bird, open forest and scrub
Black-capped Sittella, open forest
Western Thrush, open forest
Chestnut-breasted Quail-thrush, mulga and mallee
Spinifex Bird, spinifex and low scrub
Southern Scrub-robin, mulga and mallee
Black-and-white Wren, Dirk Hartog and Barrow Island
Banded Wren, forests and coastal thickets
Blue-and-white Wren, saltbush and bluebush flats
Variegated Wren, heathlands, undergrowth, low scrub
Red-winged Wren, forest undergrowth and heathlands
Southern Emu-wren, swampy heathlands
Rufous-crowned Emu-wren, spinifex
Redthroat, stunted scrub
Western Grass-wren, saltbush and spinifex
Western Warbler, open forest
Spotted Scrub-wren, dense undergrowth

Rufous Bristle-bird, low scrub
Bristle-bird, swampy heaths and scrubs
Mangrove Robin, mangroves
Scarlet Robin, forests
Red-capped Robin, inland forests and scrub
Western Yellow Robin, forests
White-breasted Robin, forests
Gilbert Whistler, inland forest and scrub
Pied Honeyeater, heaths and scrublands
Spiny-cheeked Honeyeater, open forest and scrub
Western Spinebill, banksia and eucalypt forest
Tawny-crowned Honeyeater, heath and low scrub
Crested Bellbird, open forest and scrublands
Black-throated Whipbird, mallee
Yellow-tailed Pardalote, inland dry scrub
Western Silvereye, forests and gardens
Red-eared Firetail Finch, forest and heathlands

1 Crested Tern *Sterna bergii*
RANGE coastal Australia and Tas.
HABITAT oceans, breeding on coastal islands.
COLOUR grey above, white below; crown of head and nape black.
LENGTH 17–19 in.

2 Spotted Harrier *Circus assimilis*
RANGE inland and some coastal areas of Australia; Tas.
HABITAT open country, plains, sometimes swamps and croplands.
COLOUR upper parts blue-grey, brown on facial discs; undersurface rufous brown, spotted throughout with white.
LENGTH (female) 23 in.; (male) 21 in.

3 Crested Pigeon *Ocyphaps lophotes*
RANGE widespread through inland Australia, except coastal south-west of south-east Australia.
HABITAT open country, scrublands, tree-lined watercourses.
COLOUR back bronzed-grey, head blue-grey with dark plume; wings pale brown, barred black and with a green-purple speculum; underparts pale blue-grey.
LENGTH 13 in.

4 Black Swan *Cygnus atratus*
RANGE Australia wherever conditions suit (but absent from the far north-east); also in Tas.
HABITAT freshwater swamps and lakes, as well as sea bays, estuaries and sheltered coasts.
COLOUR black, with white flight quills; beak red.
LENGTH 3 ft.

5 White-necked Heron *Ardea pacifica*

BIRDS OF THE KALGOORLIE - ALICE

Emu, plains and open forests
Wedgetail Eagle, inland plains, forests, ranges
Square-tailed Kite, inland plains and watercourses
Black-breasted Buzzard, inland plains
Grey Falcon, plains and inland ranges
Little Quail, in coveys on open plains
Red-kneed Dotterel, margins of rivers and lagoons
Banded Stilt, swamps, tidal flats, salt lakes
White-headed Stilt, shallow lakes and swamps
Plumed Pigeon, stony spinifex country
Western Plumed Pigeon, rocky, spinifex
Rose-throated Parrot, grasslands and spinifex
Port Lincoln Parrot, watercourse gums, scrublands
Naretha Parrot, scrub on Western Nullarbor
Scarlet-chested Parrot, plains and low scrub. Rare
Budgerigar, open country with occasional trees
Night Parrot, spinifex, samphire, or sandstone ranges. Rare
Black-eared Cuckoo, scattered through interior. Rare
Cave Owl, caves of the Nullarbor
Crow, ranges and inland scrub
Little Crow, inland scrubs
Mudlark, open areas, usually near water
Grey Butcher-bird, open forest and scrub
White-browed Tree-creeper, scrub-lands
White-browed Babbler, scrub and open forest
Nullarbor Quail-thrush, open plains and low scrub
Spinifex Bird, spinifex and low scrub
Rusty Field-wren, heath and low scrub
Western Grass-wren, saltbush, spinifex, low scrub
Dusky Grass-wren, porcupine-grass on ranges
Turquoise Wren, low scrub, gorges of ranges
Purple-backed Wren, low inland scrub
Whitlock Thornbill, Nullarbor Plains
Robust Thornbill, mulga scrubs
Samphire Thornbill, low bushes and samphire flats
Yellow Weebill, foliage of river gums and mallee
Western Whiteface, open scrub-lands
Chestnut-breasted Whiteface, open scrub-lands
Rufous Grass-wren, spinifex
Eyrean Grass-wren, cane grass near Lake Eyre
Willie Wagtail, open country, usually near water
Masked Wood-swallow, open forest and scrub
Little Wood-swallow, open country and ranges
White-fronted Honeyeater, low scrubs and dry heaths
Grey Honeyeater, mulga
Singing Honeyeater, scrub and open forest
Grey-headed Honeyeater, stunted eucalypts and scrub
Yellow-fronted Honeyeater, mallee and other eucalypts
Yellow-throated Miner, open forest and scrub
Crested Bellbird, open forest, mallee and mulga
Wedgebill, mulga scrub
Crimson Chat, open plains with low bushes
Orange Chat, samphire flats
Desert Chat (Gibber-bird), stony 'gibber' plains
Mistletoe Bird, eucalypts, such as river gums
Painted Finch, spinifex and grasslands
Zebra Finch, grasslands and scrub

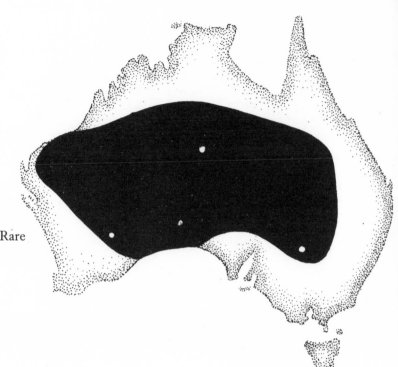

SPRINGS - BROKEN HILL REGION

1 Emu *Dromaius novae-hollandiae*
RANGE Australia generally; now extinct in
Tas., and absent from settled coastal areas
of Australia.
HABITAT Grassland-plains, mulga scrub of
open forest.
COLOUR dull grey-brown.
HEIGHT (standing upright) 5–6 ft.

2 Grey Butcher-bird *Cracticus torquatus*
RANGE mainland Australia (except the far
north) and Tas.
HABITAT open forests and woodlands.
COLOUR black and grey above, white
beneath; rump white; wings brown-grey.
LENGTH $9\frac{1}{2}$–$11\frac{1}{2}$ in.

3 Banded Stilt *Cladorhynchus leucocephalus*
RANGE southern Australia, visitor to Tas.
HABITAT tidal flats, shallow lakes, swamps;
has a preference for salt-lakes of interior.
COLOUR white except for brown-black
wings, chestnut band across the breast,
and dark line down abdomen; long legs are
pink.
LENGTH 15–18 in.

INDEX

Acanthorhynchus superciliosus, 16
Accipiter cirrocephalus, 73
Accipitridae, 42
Albatross, Shy, 66
Alcyone azurea, 2, 5
Alectura lathami, 73
Anas gibberifrons, 67; *superciliosus*, 71
Anhinga rufa, 50–1
Anseranus semipalmata, 50
Ardea novaehollandiae, 52–3; *pacifica*, 77
Artamus cinereus, 64
Atrichornis rufescens, 10–1
Australian Little Eagle, 42
Australian Pelican, 54–5

Barnardius zonarius, 40–1; *zonarius semitorquatus*, 38–9
Black Duck, 71
Black Swan, 77
Boobook Owl, 44–5
Bowerbird, Golden, 10; Great, 66–7
Brolga, 52, 73
Brush Turkey, 73
Butcher-bird, Grey, 79

Cacatua galerita, 40
Caspian Tern, 67
Charadrius cucullatus, 71; *melanops*, 52
Chat, Crimson, 30–1; Orange, 27, 30
Chlamydera nuchalis, 66–7
Circus assimilis, 77
Cladorhynchus leucocephalus, 79
Climacteris rufa, 58
Cockatiel, 40
Cockatoo, Great Palm, 75; Sulphur-crested, 40
Cormorant, Pied, 70
Cracticus torquatus, 79
Crested Tern, 77
Cuckoo-Shrike, Ground, 26–7
Cygnus atratus, 77
Cyrtostomus frenatus, 6–7

Dacelo gigas, 64–5
Darter, 50–1
Dendrocygna eytoni, 75
Dicaeum hirundinaceum, 61
Diomeda cauta, 66
Dotterel, Black-fronted, 52; Hooded, 71
Dromaius novae-hollandiae, 79

Eagle, Australian Little, 42

Egretta alba, 52; *intermedia*, 74; *garzetta*, 66
Egret, Little, 66; Plumed, 74; White, 52
Elanus notatus, 66
Emu, 79
Eolophus roseicapillus, 38
Eopsaltria chrysorrhoa, 22, 25; *griseogularis*, 22, 24
Epthianura aurifrons, 27, 30; *tricolor*, 30–1
Erolia acuminata, 71
Eudyptula minor, 67

Falco cenchroides, 42–3; *peregrinus*, 73
Falconidae, 42
Falconiformes, 42
Falcon, Peregrine, 73
Falcunculus leucogaster, 64
Fantail, Rufous, 12–3
Flycatcher, Black-faced, 8–9
Fregata minor, 75
Frigate-bird, Greater, 75

Galah, 38
Gerygone fusca, 62
Glossopsitta porphyrocephala, 36–7
Golden Whistler, 62–3
Grebe, Crested, 67
Grey Teal, 67
Grus rubicunda, 52, 73
Gull, Silver, 54

Halcyon pyrrhopygia, 32–3; *sancta*, 62
Haliaetus morphnoides, 42
Harrier, Spotted, 77
Heron, White-faced, 52–3; White-necked, 77
Himantopus leucocephalus, 70
Honeyeater, New Holland, 18; Western Spinebill, 18; Yellow-faced, 18; Yellow-plumed, 14–5
Hydroprogne caspia, 67
Hylochelidon nigricans, 60

Ibis, White, 75

Jabiru, 75

Kestrel, Nankeen, 42–3
Kingfisher, Azure, 2, 5; Red-backed, 32–3; Sacred, 62
Kite, Black-shouldered, 66
Kookaburra, Laughing, 64–5

Larus novaehollandiae, 54
Loriidae, 34
Lorikeet, Purple-crowned, 36–7; Rainbow, 37; Scaly-breasted, 34

Magpie Geese, 50
Malurinae, 46
Malurus cyaneus, 48; *cyanotus*, 48; *elegans*, 48–9; *lamberti*, 48; *melanocephalus*, 46–7; *splendens*, 48
Martin, Tree, 60
Meliornis novae-hollandiae 2
Meliphaga chrysops, 18; *ornata*, 14–5
Meliphagidae, 14–9
Menura superba, 71
Merops ornatus, 28–9
Miner, Yellow-throated, 16–7
Mistletoe Bird, 61
Monarcha melanopsis, 8–9
Muscicapidae, 20
Muscicapinae, 20
Myzantha flavigula, 16–7

Nankeen Night-Heron, 73
Nectariniidae, 6
Neophema pulchella, 34–5
Neositta pileata, 67
Night-Heron, Nankeen, 73
Ninox novaeseelandiae, 44–5
Nycticorax caledonicus, 73
Nymphicus hollandicus, 40

Ocyphaps lophotes, 77
Oriole, Olive-backed, 58–9
Oriolus sagittatus, 58–9
Owl, Boobook, 44–5; Masked, 45

Pachycephala pectoralis, 62
Pandionidae, 42
Pardalote, Red-browed, 64; Spotted, 60; Striated, 60–1
Pardalotus punctatus, 60; *rubricatus*, 64; *substriatus*, 60–1
Parrot, Mulga, 40; Port Lincoln, 40–1; Red-capped, 40; Turquoise, 34–5; Twenty-eight, 38–9
Pelecanus conspicillatus, 54–5
Pelican, Australian, 54–5
Penguin, Fairy, 67
Peregrine Falcon, 73
Petroica goodenovii, 22; *phoenicea*, 20
Phaethon rubricauda, 56–7
Phalacrocorax varius, 70
Pigeon, Crested, 77
Platalea flavipes, 71; *regia*, 73
Platycercus elegans, 36–7; *icterotis*, 38
Plover, Banded, 73
Podiceps cristatus, 67
Priondura newtoniana, 10

Probosciger aterrimus, 75
Procellariiformes, 54
Psephotus varius, 40
Psittacidae, 34
Psittaciformes, 42
Psophodes olivaceus, 6
Pteropodocys maxima, 26–7
Purpureicephalus spurius, 40

Rainbow Bird, 28–9
Rhipidura rufifrons, 12–3
Robin, Flame, 20; Red-capped, 22–3; Scarlet, 20–1; Northern Yellow, 22, 25; Western Yellow, 22, 24
Rosella, Crimson, 36–7; Western, 38

Sacred Kingfisher, 62
Sandpiper, Sharp-tailed, 71
Scrub-bird, Rufous, 10–1
Scrub-Wren, Yellow-throated, 12–3
Sericornis lathami, 12–3
Shriketit, Western, 64
Sittella, Black-capped, 67
Sparrowhawk, Collared, 73
Spinebill, Western, 16
Spoonbill, Royal, 73; Yellow-billed, 71
Sterna bergii, 77
Stilt, White-headed, 70; Banded, 79
Strigidae, 42
Sunbird, Yellow-breasted, 6–7
Superb Lyrebird, 71

Tern, Caspian, 67; Crested, 77
Threskiornis molucca, 75
Tree-creeper, Rufous, 58
Tree-Duck, Plumed, 75
Tree Martin, 60
Trichoglossus chlorolepidotus, 34; *haematodus*, 37
Tropic bird, Red-tailed, 56–7
Tytonidae, 42

Warbler, Western, 62
Western Shriketit, 64
Whipbird, Eastern, 6
Whistler, Golden, 62–3
White Ibis, 75
Woodswallow, Black-faced, 64
Wren, Banded, 48; Blue-and-white, 48; Red-backed, 46–7; Red-winged, 48–9; Splendid, 48; Variegated, 48

Xenorhynchus asiaticus, 75

Zonifer tricolor, 73

SELECTED BIBLIOGRAPHY

A. Landsborough Thomson, (Ed.) *A New Dictionary of Birds* (Nelson, 1966).

Austin, O. L., and Singer, A., *Birds of the World* (Paul Hamlyn, London, 1961).

Bourke, P. A., *Elementary Bird Study* (Paterson Brokensha Pty Ltd, Perth, 1955).

Fleay, D., *Nightwatchmen of Bush and Plain* (Jacaranda Press, Brisbane, 1968).

Forshaw, J. M., *Australian Parrots* (Lansdowne Press, 1969).

Frith, H. J., *The Mallee Fowl* (Angus and Robertson, Ltd, Sydney, 1962).

Frith, H. J., *Waterfowl in Australia* (Angus and Robertson Ltd, Sydney, 1967).

Frith, H. J., (Ed.) *Birds in the Australian High Country* (A. H. & A. W. Reed, Sydney, 1969).

Immelmann, K., *Australian Finches in Bush and Aviary* (Angus & Robertson Ltd, 1965).

Marshal, A. J., *Bower Birds* (Oxford University Press, 1954).

Officer, H. R., *Australian Honeyeaters* (Bird Observers' Club, Melbourne, 1964).

Officer, H. R., *Australian Flycatchers and their Allies* (Bird Observers' Club, 1969).

Serventy, D. L., and Whittell, H. M., *Birds of Western Australia* (Lamb Publications Pty Ltd, Perth, 1967).

Slater, P., and others, *A Field Guide To Australian Birds* (Rigby Ltd, Adelaide, 1970).

Smith, L. H., *The Lyrebird* (Lansdowne Press, Melbourne, 1968).

Van Tyne, J., and Berger, A. J., *Fundamentals of Ornithology* (Wiley, 1961).

Whittell, H. M., *The Literature of Australian Birds* (Paterson Brokensha, 1954).